WITHDRAWN

NO WAY!

WITHDRAWN

ODD MEDICAL CURES

Michael J. Rosen

and Ben Kassoy

Illustrations by Pat Sandy

M Millbrook Press • Minneapolis

Millbrook Press
A division of Lerner Publishing Group, Inc.
241 First Avenue North
Minneapolis, MN 55401 U.S.A.

Website address: www.lernerbooks.com

Main body text set in Adrianna Regular 12/16
Typeface provided by Chank

Rosen, Michael J., 1954-
    Odd medical cures / by Michael J. Rosen and Ben Kassoy ; illustrated by Pat Sandy.
        p.   cm. — (No way!)
    Includes index.
    ISBN 978-0-7613-8987-3 (lib. bdg. : alk. paper)
    ISBN 978-1-4677-1706-9 (eBook)
    1. Medicine—Juvenile literature. 2. Traditional medicine—Juvenile literature. I. Kassoy, Ben. II. Sandy, Pat, illustrator. III. Title.
R133.5.R68 2014
615.8'8—dc23   2012042372

Manufactured in the United States of America
1 – BP – 7/15/13

The authors would like to recognize the generous contribution of Christoffer Strömstedt, as well as the efforts of Ashley Heestand, Colin Stoecker, and Claire Hamilton in the researching, fact-checking, and drafting of the No Way! series of books.

The images in this book are used with the permission of: © Bettmann/COR-BIS, p. 5 (left); © Copyright by Harris Graber/Flickr Open/Getty Images, p. 5 (right); © Amazon-Images/Alamy, p. 6; © Volker Steger/Photo Researchers, Inc., p. 7; AFP/Getty Images/Newscom, p. 8; © iStockphoto.com/Omar Ariff, p. 9; REUTERS/Ajay Verma (Indian Health Society), p. 10; Wikimedia Commons, p. 13; Mast Irham/EPA/Newscom, p. 15; Charles Trainor Jr. KRT/Newscom, p. 17 (right); © iStockphoto/Thinkstock, p. 17 (left); Bettmann/Corbis/AP Images, p. 19 (top); deepestbluesea/Wikimedia Commons, p. 19 (bottom); © David J. Green/Alamy, p. 20; © China Photos/Stringer/Getty Images, p. 21; © Patrice Latron/Look At Sciences/Science Photo Library/Photo Researchers, Inc., p. 22; John Giles/PA Wire via AP Images, p. 23; Wellcome Library, London, p. 24; STR/EPA/Newscom, p. 26; © Westend61/Getty Images, p. 27; © Caroline von Tuempling/Iconica/Getty Images, p. 29.
Front cover: © Kevin Schafer/Alamy.

TABLE of CONTENTS

DON'T-TRY-IT DIETS
WEIGHT LOSS SCHEMES

Throughout history, people have tried strange schemes to shed pounds. Were these dieters losing weight? Or just losing their minds?

SLIMMING SOAP

You can wash off germs and filth. But what about getting rid of fat and flab? In the 1920s and the 1930s, some people lathered up with "reducing" soaps such as Fatoff or Fat-O-No. These suds claimed to "magically wash away flabby arms and love handles!" The results? Let's say using the soaps worked as well as rubbing a dictionary on your head to get smarter.

BLUE FOOD

Restaurants use the colors red and yellow to make people hungrier.

Scientists say that blue has the opposite effect. So a Japanese company once tried to sell dieting glasses with blue-tinted lenses. People may have eaten less blue—*eew*-looking—food. But they also got headaches and looked silly. After a while, dieters ditched the specs.

FLETCHERiZiNG

Horace Fletcher once said, "Nature will castigate those who don't masticate." (*Masticate* is a fancier word for chewing. *Castigate* means "to reject.") Translation: Chew food thoroughly before swallowing.

During the early 1900s, many people took Fletcher's tips on food. His Fletcherizing diet told dieters to tilt their heads forward and chew every bite thirty-two times. Then, head tilted backward, dieters could swallow whatever dripped down the throat. They spat out the rest.

So much for table manners.

Blue? Eww! Does a blue tint make this meal less appetizing?

SHOO, FLY! WAIT—COME BACK! MAGGOT THERAPY

The botfly is a nasty pest with a taste for human flesh—and for bacon.

Botflies are insects that can make your skin crawl. Botfly larvae (newborns) burrow deep within human flesh. Boils form on the skin as the larvae feast on their host. (That would be you.)

Want to uninvite these disgusting diners? Serve yourself a side of bacon! Rub bacon on your sores, and these nasty nibblers will pop up for a taste. When they do, doctors can pluck them from the skin with tweezers. Oil, butter, and chewing gum also do the trick.

These surgical maggots clean wounds by eating dead skin.

You've said, "Shoo, fly!" to botfly larvae. But you might want another type of baby fly to stick around. Believe it or not, flesh-eating maggots are mini medical miracles!

Maggot therapy has a long history. Many cultures have used these insects to heal wounds during wartime. The famous French general Napoleon relied on larvae. So did soldiers in the U.S. Civil War (1861–1865). Even the modern U.S. government has OK'd maggot therapy.

How does it work? To a maggot, *living* skin is yucky, but dead skin is *yummy!* (Humans, beware of zombies! Zombies, beware of maggots!) Set maggots on a wound, and they'll devour the dead, dirty flesh. After forty-eight hours of feasting, they will have cleaned your wound! Maggots also leave behind chemicals that help new skin cells grow. Bye-bye, germs. Hello, beautiful skin!

So what's the lesson here? Skin with botflies? Bring on the bacon! Skin with wounds? Bring on the maggots!

THiS MAY STiNG A LiTTLE
VENOM THERAPY

It's a summer day. You're enjoying a family picnic. And you're probably hoping that bees mind their own beeswax. But some people get stung on purpose. Why? A sting may make you yelp, but it can also be of help.

A bee's venom carries melittin (meh-LIH-tihn). This toxin can kill germs and prevent your skin from swelling. It can take the *ouch!* out of an injury.

A patient in China undergoes bee venom therapy—but he doesn't look happy about it.

Melittin has many uses. The disease multiple sclerosis can harm people's vision and affect their movements. Bee venom can improve sight and coordination. For patients whose bones ache, melittin makes the pain buzz off.

Sure, bee venom can be blended into a cream. But to really stop pain, nature's way is best. Bring on the sting! Yes, getting melittin from a stinger may hurt. But a little pain now can prevent a lot of pain later.

Nature has some other cures you'd be likely to run from. Venom from a snakebite may end your life— or save it. The toxin in a king cobra's bite is strong enough to kill twenty people. But a tiny amount of that same venom can reduce aches and throbs. Some doctors claim that the copperhead snake's venom has even stopped some cancers from spreading.

STRiNGiNG YOURSELF ALONG
SUTRA NETi

Parents, teachers, or anyone with sense will tell you the same thing. "Don't put that—whatever it is—up your nose!" Anyone but a yoga master.

Yoga is a form of exercise that links breathing, movement, and well-being. For centuries, some yoga masters have been sliding strings up their noses. This is known as sutra neti. It can help with a host of health problems. You just have to know how to hose the nose.

Don't let this advice go in one ear and out the other. It's supposed to go into your nostril! And don't try this at home—unless your neighbor happens to be a yoga expert! Here's how sutra neti works.

Sutra neti is like nostril flossing. You need string, an open nose, and an open mind.

Grab a string. Cotton dipped in beeswax is best. Take good care of it, and you can use the same string for a month. Reduce, reuse, re-nostril!

If you've ever laughed so hard that milk sprayed out your sniffer, you know that pathways connect your mouth and your nose. So thread the string into your nose. Reach into your throat and grab it with your fingers. Then slowly floss back and forth.

Sutra neti will clear up the spaces behind your nose, cheeks, and eyes. Your runny nose will run away! According to the masters, "Soon, the misty and mysterious dark cave will become a bright and clear one."

Sutra neti also triggers nerves in the brain. After all, your whole body's connected. You may become more alert. You might also have fewer headaches or even improve your vision.

GOOD VIBRATIONS RADIONICS

Albert Abrams was the creator of radionics. In the early 1900s, he used vibrations (back-and-forth movements) and energy to "diagnose" and "treat" thousands of patients. Abrams would start by thumping a patient's belly so it shook. He would hold a jar of diseased human tissue to the patient's forehead. If the sound of the thumping changed, Abrams claimed the person was ill.

Next, Abrams would hook up the patient to his Dynamizer. This machine supposedly measured a person's energy. Abrams said that the machine could figure out the type of disease and its location. When "bad energy" (sickness) showed up, Abrams sent an electric current through the patient's body. He claimed this "retuned" the person's bad vibrations. Go, Dynamizer, go!

Albert Abrams was a schemer first, scientist second.

Abrams boasted that he could diagnose patients from afar. People from all over the world sent him samples of their blood. Abrams said he could use the blood to figure out a person's illness. He said he could predict age, race, and gender too. Abrams once diagnosed a patient with three separate problems: cancer, strep throat, and a sinus infection!

There was one problem. The blood was a guinea pig's. A guinea pig that didn't have cancer. Or strep. Or sinus trouble. The American Medical Association had sent the sample as a trick. It turns out that Abrams's Dynamizer could hardly detect energy waves, much less send out good vibrations. Its switches and gadgets were just for show. Radionics was a proven scam.

THAT'S SHOCKING!
ELECTRIC THERAPY

You know not to plug something in near a bathtub full of water. And you know not to stick your finger in a light socket. But here's some shocking news. Electricity can also make you feel better.

The ancient Romans placed electric eels on the heads of patients. Why? To treat headaches and mental illnesses! The eels would send mild electric charges through a patient's body. How was the brain being affected by the shocks? The Romans didn't know. Still, eels seemed to work better than kittens or seagulls.

This woman from Indonesia hopes to get a healthful buzz from electrified rails.

Speaking of shocking: Legend tells of a Chinese man who placed himself across the tracks of a nearby train. He was unable to move his legs. He had decided to end his life. But before the train arrived, the electrified rails cured him. He could walk! Since then, dozens of people throughout Asia have taken to the tracks. They believe in the power of voltage!

So is this jolt a joke? Well, an electric current does pass along one of the metal rails on a train's tracks. That current also pulses through the body of anyone touching the rails. Many people claim the current has helped cure high blood pressure, sleeplessness, and even diabetes. But medical experts say these "patients" are way off track. No benefits from this "track therapy" have been proven. Are these locomotive lovers just *loco*?

POISON ... POIS-OFF!
CHELATION

You may love rock 'n' roll. But be careful of heavy metals. Let's say you breathe in lead-based paint. Or you touch mercury from a broken thermometer. Even tiny bits of these metals are poisonous! That's nothing to sing about.

Chelation (kee-LAY-shun) therapy removes poison metals from the body. *Chelation* comes from *chela*, the Greek word for *claw*. During this treatment, a doctor injects a liquid mix of chemicals into your bloodstream. Think of scuba-diving cops on a high-speed chase through your body. They're tracking down the poison metals and cuffing them! Together they zoom right out of the body—through your pee. *Urine* jail!

A patient in Florida tries chelation therapy through an intravenous (into the vein) drip.

Could these foot pads take away toxins?

Chelation therapy is a proven treatment for poisoning from metals such as lead, iron, and arsenic. Some fans of chelation claim that it also treats illnesses such as multiple sclerosis, cancer, and heart disease. It makes sense. What happens if someone eats too many donuts or cheese curls? Fat builds up in the bloodstream. That creates heart disease. So can't some squad of chelating cops bust those sugary criminals? The jury (science) is still out.

Here's another kooky kind of chelation. Some people tape footpads filled with minerals and dried wood vinegar to their feet every night. Upon waking, these folks find that the pads are gray and blotchy. So are the pads full of the toxins that got sucked out? Well, doctors say it's the people that are full of it! Exposed to moisture (like foot sweat), the vinegar mix turns gray or brown.

QUACK IS WHACK
QUACKERY

When it comes to medicine, *quack* has nothing to do with ducks. No, a quack is a cheater. Quacks make wild scientific claims using fake chemistry. In the Middle Ages, quacks said they could cure people hit by a deadly plague. They treated patients with duck beaks stuffed with herbs. It didn't exactly work.

In 1647 a medicine called Daffy's Elixir appeared in Britain. Thomas Daffy claimed his medicine could cure nearly every illness. The elixir was loaded with "natural" ingredients such as licorice, raisins, and alcohol. But these ingredients mostly helped patients poop, not heal.

Unlike another famous Daffy, Thomas Daffy wasn't a duck. But he was a total quack. Hmmm. It *does* sound like medical quacks and ducks are related. But the term actually comes from a Dutch word, *kwakzalver* (QUAK-zahl-verr). This word means a seller of medical ointments.

In modern times, *quack* means a person who sells products or treatments that are worthless in treating illnesses. Fakers continue to quack away on late-night commercials. You can read their pitches on the Internet. The U.S. Food and Drug Administration offers tips for spotting these frauds.

• Watch for products that claim to cure a wide range of illnesses. A single pill can cure "arthritis, a runny nose, and diabetes"? Not likely.

• Be doubtful of "instant" cures. "This cream cures allergies in days!" Two days? Two thousand days? Hmm … doesn't say.

• "Natural" doesn't always mean better. Poisonous mushrooms are "natural." But would you eat them?

BURN, BABY, BURN! MOXiBUSTiON, EAR CANDLiNG, AND FiRE CUPPiNG

Here are three fiery treatments that the devil might have pulled from his doctor's kit.

MOXiBUSTiON

In the Asian practice of moxibustion (mahx-ih-BUHS-chuhn), healers grind up a plant called mugwort. Then they light it and place the burned-up remains on a patient's skin. Heat created by the mugwort sinks deep within the body. This treatment relieves tiredness, joint pain, and stomach problems. Need proof? Talk to the twenty-five hundred years' worth of patients who say they've been healed.

EAR CANDLiNG

Use care when poking a cotton swab inside your ear. Use *extra* care when you're holding a lit candle. In ear candling, a person places one end of a hollow candle within the ear canal. Fire burns at the other end. Healers say that the heat draws wax and toxins from the body right out of the ear. But the U.S. Food and Drug Administration says these people are just playing with fire.

FiRE CUPPiNG

Fire cupping is another ancient tradition that modern science questions. It's supposed to improve blood flow, help breathing, and reduce pain. First, a healer dips a cotton swab in alcohol. Then the swab's set on fire. The flame is held inside a bell-shaped cup. Finally, the hot cup goes on a patient's skin. The healer does this with about a dozen more cups.

As the cups cool down, they create a vacuum on the patient's skin. The skin swells up inside each cup. Healers say that harmful toxins get sucked out too. After twenty minutes or so, the cups come off. But bruises or even burns may stick around.

The heat is on: a man in China lies down for some fire cupping.

CHiLLY THRiLLS
CRYOGENICS

With cryogenics, the future is now. And it's very cold.

Science fiction has probably introduced you to cryogenics (kreye-oh-JEH-nihks). Someone is frozen in an icy liquid. Years later, the body thaws out. The person starts a new life ... *in the future.*

Sorry. Cryogenics doesn't really work that way. But it does work!

Strip down to nothing but a bathing suit. Actually, you'll want socks and gloves too. They hold off frostbite from what happens next.

Step into the cryogenic chamber. It's like a giant freezer ... but colder. This chilly chamber drops 120 degrees below zero (-84°C)! If you can handle the weather for about three teeth-chattering minutes, you'll come out refreshed. Low temperatures cause the body to release chemicals called endorphins (ehn-DOHR-fihns). These chemicals ease pain and stress.

Athletes who score big under pressure are said to have ice water in their veins. But one key to success may be actual ice water. Cold tubs and ice baths are popular in locker rooms throughout the wide world of sports.

Athletes have weird ways of describing their postgame soaks. *It's super cold. It's a deep burn. It hurts so good!* But athletes and trainers agree on the ice bath's perks. Ice water tightens blood vessels and drains blood from the limbs. This gives athletes more energy. It helps prevent injuries and cramps. It makes for quicker recoveries. And it's the one thing that will make a 300-pound (136-kilogram) football lineman squeal at a touch.

GO WITH THE FLOW
PHLEBOTOMY

In the 1800s, English "healers" used this tool for bloodletting.

You'd go to the doctor if you were bleeding. But for twenty-five hundred years, people went to the doctor *in order* to bleed. Phlebotomy (fleh-BAH-toh-mee) is a "treatment" that's also known as bloodletting. A healer would tie a tight bandage around a patient's limb. This binding ensured that only blood from that part of the body could be drained. Passing out was a sign of success!

Healers believed bloodletting treated nearly everything. Back pain? Lose blood! Fever? Slice a vein!

Early on, healers believed that spilled blood let out evil spirits. Later, healers believed bloodletting released infected or "bad blood." Others believed that fluids in the bodies of the ill were out of whack. They thought draining blood would restore the balance.

To drain small amounts of blood, healers put aside their knives. They used leeches instead. Yes, bloodsucking worms would, well, suck out the bad blood.

Healers practiced weird methods of bloodletting around the world. Ancient peoples from Egypt to Greece to China let it flow. In medieval Europe, barber and surgeon were basically the same job. So barbers practiced bloodletting! Shave, haircut, vein cut . . .

Phlebotomy was so common in 1799 that doctors treated former president George Washington for a sore throat with four bloodletting sessions. Losing half of his blood didn't help Washington. His throat swelled until he could no longer breathe.

The practice didn't die down until the 1800s. Scientists such as Louis Pasteur revealed that germs, not unbalanced fluid levels, cause disease.

MESSY MEDICINE
MUD BATHS AND HAY BATHS

Splash! This young girl takes a dip in volcanic mud near Russia's Sea of Azov.

Pigs love to mess around in mud. Don't say "yuck!" The muck helps keep them cool. And it turns out that mud has benefits for humans too.

About eight million years ago, Mount Konocti erupted. This volcano is nestled in modern Castiloga, California. Mount Konocti covered the land there with volcanic ash. Fast-forward to the nineteenth century. Native Americans known as the Wappo began soaking themselves in the ancient ash. The grungy stuff cleared their pores. It removed toxins. It also eased pain. The Wappo got down and dirty. They rose up happy and healthy!

People in modern times dip themselves in all sorts of soils to feel better. Warm mud relieves stress. Up to your neck in frustration? Then get up to your neck in a mud bath!

While some people play piggy to relax, others play horsey! The country of Austria is known for its famous hay baths. Sound itchy and uncomfortable? The hay is freshly cut and steam-heated to more than 100°F (38°C). That heat makes it soft and moist. People add wildflowers for a refreshing scent.

Hay bathers are wrapped inside a blanket of the stuff. Then an extra blanket of hay is heaped on top. The heat from the bath eases pain. It also improves breathing and blood flow. Here's how one patient described a hay bath. It's like being covered "in warmth and breathing in the light scent of cut grass and wild flowers." Think that's something you'd ever say after visiting a doctor?

ROCK OUT!
CRYSTAL AND GEMSTONE THERAPIES

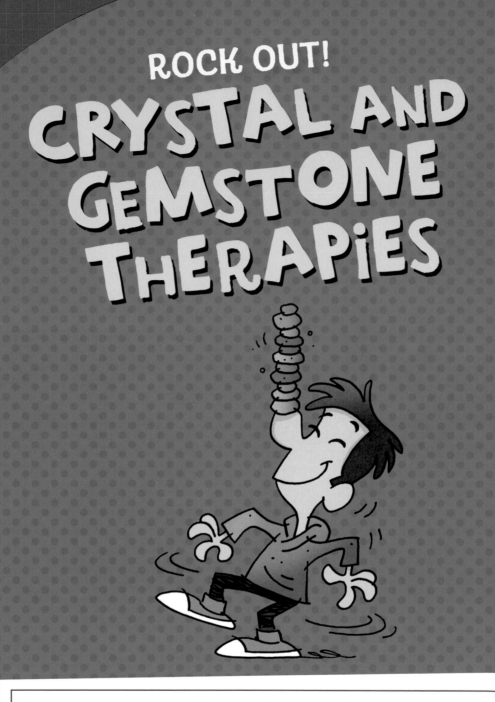

Rocks have many uses. They can become buildings. Or paper weights. Or jewelry. And according to ancient texts and modern-day believers, rocks can also heal pain and illness.

Crystal therapy is linked to the Hindu idea of chakras (CHAH-krahs). Hindu tradition says that chakras are places where the body collects energy. Some Hindus believe that placing a crystal of the right color near its chakra can boost a patient's health. For

Fans of crystal therapy believe a crystal in the right place can improve a person's health.

example, a cough might mean that a throat chakra is blocked. So a healer places a blue-green crystal on the patient's throat. Sore no more!

The heart chakra is tied to heartaches. Crystal healers use rose quartz crystals to get people pumped up again. To cure headaches or to boost brainpower, healers use amethyst crystals on a person's crown (head) chakra.

Gemstone therapy goes even further. These healers claim that the seven colors of the rainbow match up with seven systems of the human body. All you need is a rock of the right color to fix the part that's ailing. Muscle trouble? You need the red light of a ruby. Brain pain? Go for the emerald's green power. Got some bad blood? Go blue! Gemstone healers use the blue sapphire to heal the circulatory system.

These healers also say that wearing the right stones on or near the matching body part helps wellness. For gemstone healers, jewelry isn't just an accessory. It's a necessity! It's not just fashion. It's medicine!

GLOSSARY

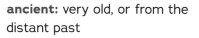

ancient: very old, or from the distant past

chakra: in Hindu tradition, one of seven "wheels" or energy centers in the body

circulatory system: the body's system of blood, blood vessels, and the heart

diagnose: to figure out what illness a patient has or what the cause of a problem is

ear canal: the passage from the outer ear to the eardrum

elixir: a sweet-tasting liquid swallowed to treat illness

endorphin: a chemical the body produces to reduce the feeling of pain

erupt: to burst or explode

heavy metal: a metal such as copper, mercury, lead, and cadmium, which are toxic to living beings

Hindu: relating to a religion and a philosophy practiced in India and elsewhere

larvae: the birth form of an insect. A larvae's body will change as it becomes an adult.

loco: in the Spanish language, "crazy"

maggot: a legless larva of certain flies or mosquitoes

subzero: a temperature that is below zero degrees

therapy: a treatment meant to cure a physical, medical, or behavioral problem

toxin: a harmful substance made by a living thing

tradition: a belief or practice that has been passed down for generations

vacuum: an emptiness of space, or sucking effect

yoga: a form of exercise that helps people become related and fit. Yoga comes from Hindu tradition.

SOURCE NOTES

5   Katherine Harmon, "Chew on This: More Mastication Cuts Calorie Intake by 12 Percent," *Scientific American,* August 3, 2011, http://blogs.scientificamerican.com/observations/2011/08/03/chew-on-this-more-mastication-cuts-calorie-intake-by-12-percent/ (February 5, 2012).

27   http://passionfortheplanet.blogspot.com/2010/03/how-haystack-can-help-heal-your-back.html (February 5, 2012).

FURTHER READING

BOOKS

Ballen, Karen Gunnison. *Seven Wonders of Medicine.* Minneapolis: Twenty-First Century Books, 2010.
Check out this book from the Seven Wonders series. It explores medical breakthroughs such as microscopes, antibiotics, and transplants.

Jacobson, Ryan. *Marvelous Medical Inventions.* Minneapolis: Lerner Publications Company, 2014.
This book in the Awesome Inventions You Use Every Day series covers many amazing tools and treatments that can save human lives.

WEBSITES

KidsHealth—For Kids
http://kidshealth.org/kid/
This fun site from KidsHealth has fact sheets, quizzes, movies, and more. The site's pages cover everything from medical terms to how the body works. Learn more about topics from illness and feelings to safety and injuries.

Science Kids—Human Body for Kids
http://www.sciencekids.co.nz/humanbody.html
This site includes games, experiments, science-fair projects, fascinating facts, cool videos, and challenging quizzes! Have fun while learning more about the human body.

INDEX